BookLife
PUBLISHING

©2020
BookLife Publishing Ltd.
King's Lynn
Norfolk, PE30 4LS

ISBN: 978-1-78637-965-8

Written by:
Mignonne Gunasekara

Edited by:
John Wood

Designed by:
Brandon Mattless

A catalogue record for this book is available from the British Library.

To use the QR code in this book, a grown-up will need to set one of these apps as the default browser on the device you are using:

- Chrome
- Safari
- Firefox
- Ecosia

PHOTO CREDITS

Images are courtesy of Shutterstock.com. With thanks to Getty Images, Thinkstock Photo and iStockphoto.

Cover – LightField Studios, Serg64. Recurring Images (cover and internals) – ilkayalptekin (background pattern), The_Pixel (grid), balabolk (headers and vectors), wildfloweret (boxes), Steve Paint (arrows), yana shypova (speech bubbles), Tsaranna (vector frames and boxes). p4–5 – Piyawat Nandeenopparit, Nataliia K, Dmitry Zimin, Mike McDonald, ace03 p6-7 – Patrick Foto, Roupplar, Purino p8-9 – Patrick Foto, Pushish Images, ANURAK PONGPATIMET p10-11 – Big Blu Books p14-15 – Benjamin Simeneta, Mihai Simonia p16-17 – CCat82, Hannamariah p18-19 – Zick Svift, michelmond, Tom Wang, Vladimir_Sotnichenko, BigKhem p22-23 – Mike McDonald

CONTENTS

Words that look like this can be found in the glossary on page 24.

Hello, SCIENTISTS!

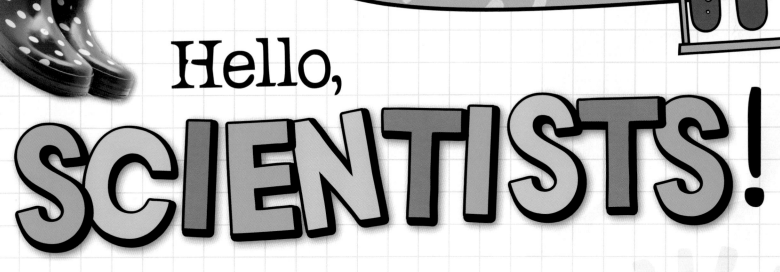

Science is about learning why and how everything works. A scientist's job is to find the answers to those questions.

WEATHER

Science can teach us about the weather. We will carry out a couple of fun <u>experiments</u> as we go.

Complete the experiments and you will earn your Weather Badge!

Let's get started!

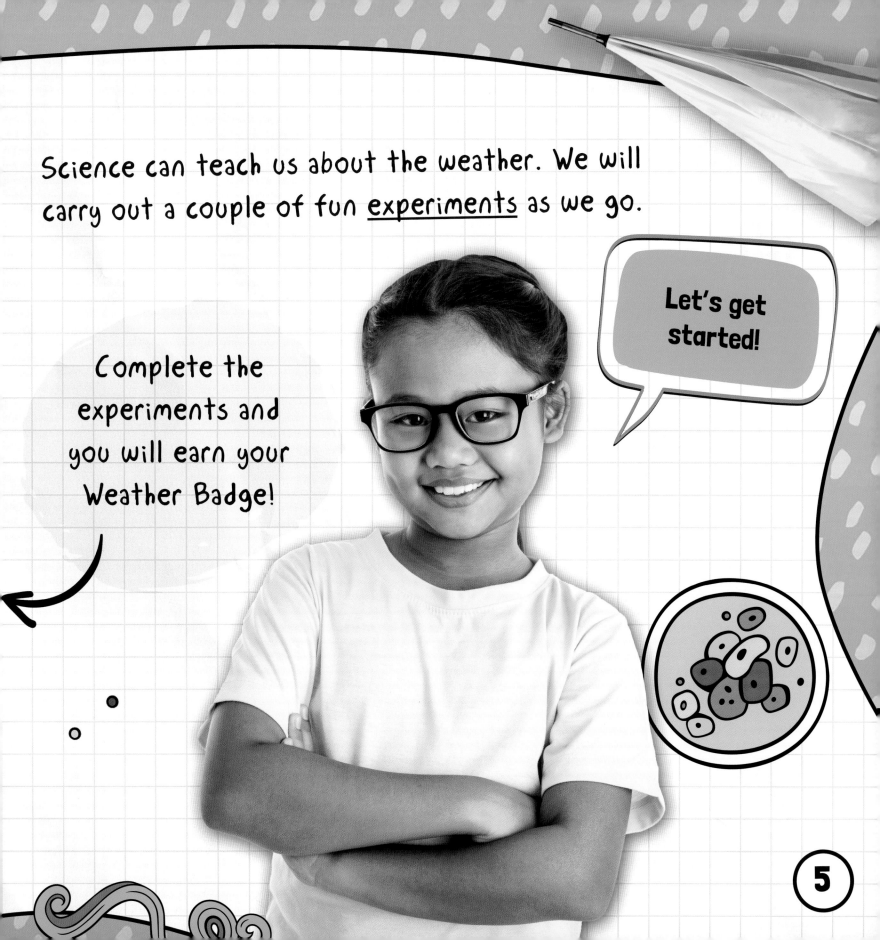

What Is WEATHER?

Weather is what it's like outside. Is it hot or cold? Windy or cloudy? Rainy or dry? These are all different types of weather.

We use temperature to talk about how hot or cold something is.

Weather is different from place to place. It also changes based on the time of day and time of year. It can be sunny in the morning but raining by the afternoon!

Check your local <u>weather forecast</u> so you can get ready for the weather.

RAIN and SNOW

Clouds are made of tiny water droplets, high in the sky. When the water droplets in the clouds get too heavy, they fall to the ground. This is rain!

When it's sunny and rainy at the same time, you might see **rainbows**.

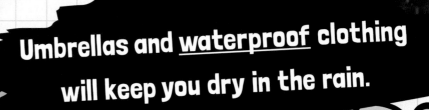

Umbrellas and <u>waterproof</u> clothing will keep you dry in the rain.

When it is cold, raindrops become <u>frozen</u> while still in the sky, and fall as snowflakes or hail.

You should wear warm clothing such as coats, scarves and gloves to stay warm in cold weather.

Experiment: Let it RAIN

Let's make a rain gauge! We can use it to measure how much rain falls in a certain amount of time.

You will need:
- An empty 2-litre plastic bottle
- Scissors
- Duct tape
- A waterproof marker
- Pebbles
- Water
- A ruler
- A notebook

1) Cut off the top of the water bottle where it becomes narrow.

2) Fill the uneven bottom of the bottle with pebbles.

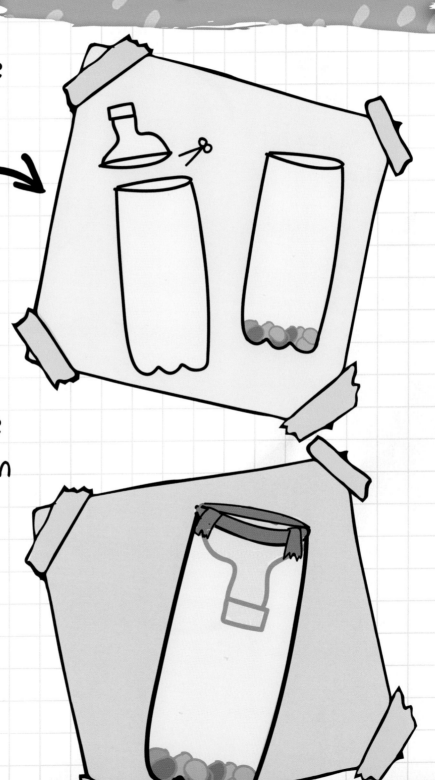

3) Take the part of the bottle you cut off, turn it upside down, and place it at the top of your gauge. Tape the edges of both pieces together. Now your gauge has a funnel.

11

4) Stick a piece of duct tape along the bottle, from the bottom to the top.

5) Draw a line next to the top of the pebbles and label this 0. Now use a ruler to mark a <u>scale</u> in centimetres on the tape.

6) Fill the bottom of the bottle with water so that it is in line with the 0 mark on your scale.

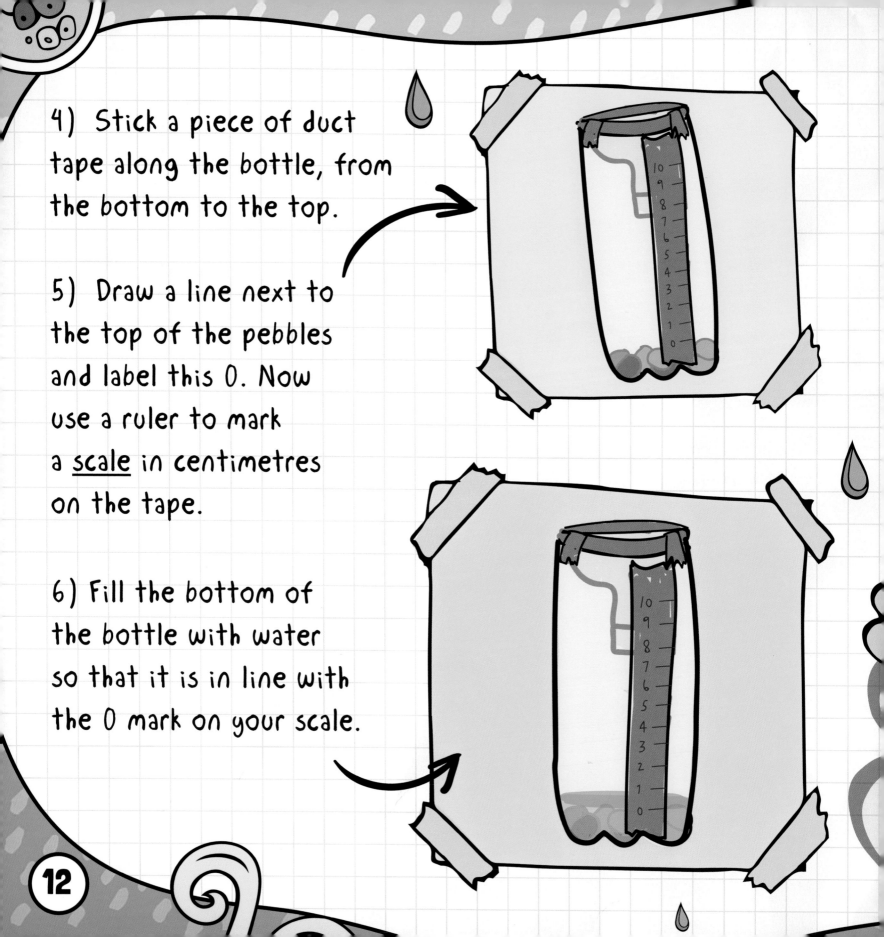

7) Put your rain gauge outside in a flat, open space.

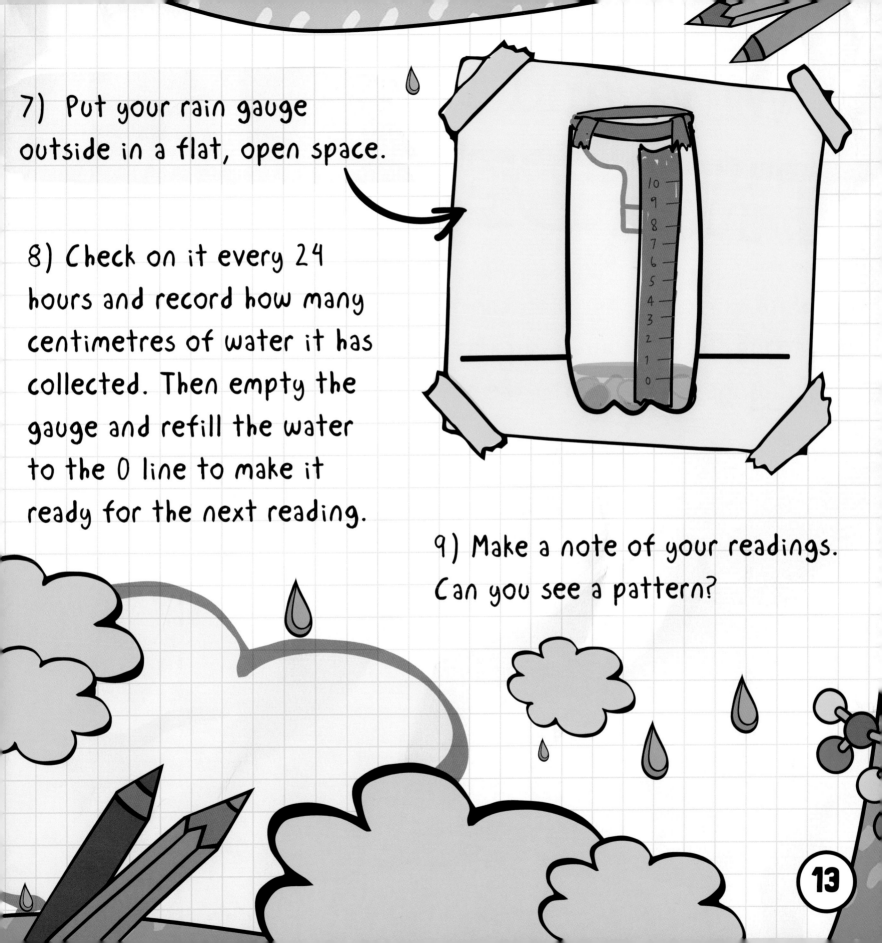

8) Check on it every 24 hours and record how many centimetres of water it has collected. Then empty the gauge and refill the water to the 0 line to make it ready for the next reading.

9) Make a note of your readings. Can you see a pattern?

Wind and THUNDERSTORMS

Wind is moving air. You can't see it, but it can be very strong. Strong winds such as <u>tornadoes</u> can lift trees, buildings and cars into the air. This causes a lot of damage.

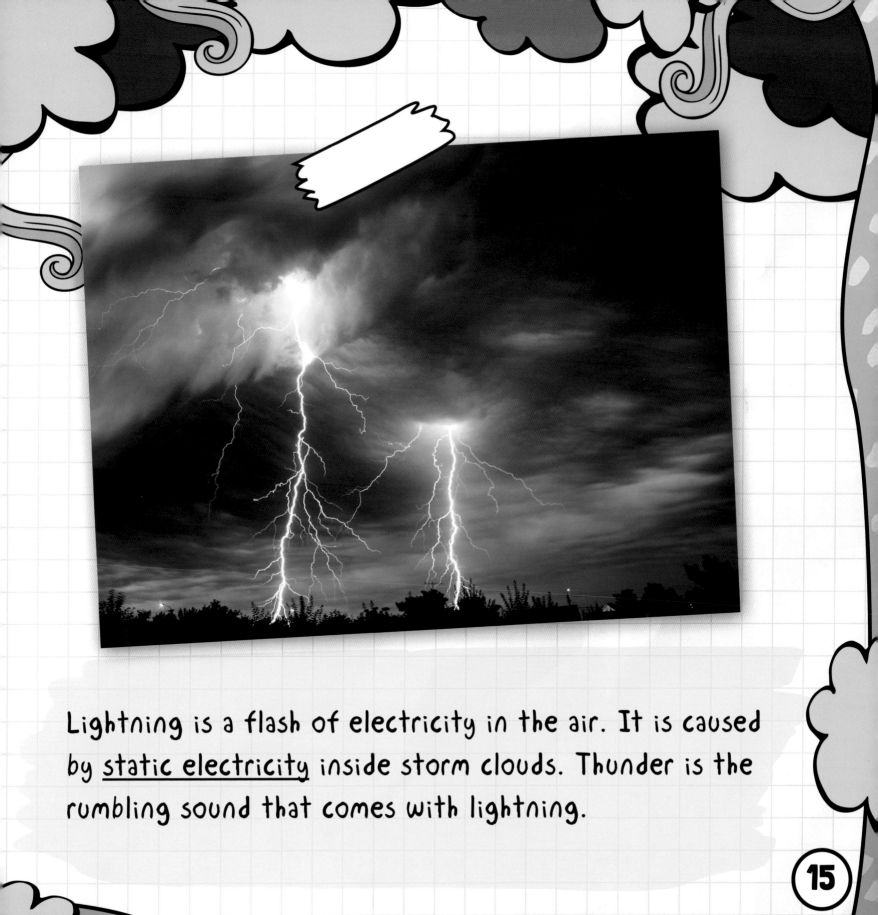

Lightning is a flash of electricity in the air. It is caused by <u>static electricity</u> inside storm clouds. Thunder is the rumbling sound that comes with lightning.

The Four SEASONS

Many countries have four seasons: spring, summer, autumn and winter. It is normally sunniest and warmest in summer. It is usually darkest and coldest in winter. There may also be snow in winter.

There are more hours of daylight in summer than there are in winter.

A field looks very different in summer and winter.

In autumn, it starts to get colder. Leaves on trees turn brown and fall off. In spring, it starts to get warmer. Flowers grow and <u>bloom</u>.

Spring

Summer

Winter

Autumn

Wacky WEATHER

Drought

Flooding

If it rains very heavily, there may be flooding. Flooding destroys <u>habitats</u> and homes. If there isn't enough rain, there may be droughts. During a drought, rivers and lakes dry up, and plants and animals might go thirsty.

Blizzards are very heavy snowstorms with strong winds that blow snow around, making it hard to see. When it is very hot for a few days, we call it a heatwave. Heatwaves can be dangerous.

Stay <u>hydrated</u> in hot weather!

Experiment: BREEZING Through

Let's make a windsock! It will tell us which direction the wind is blowing from.

You will need:
- The sleeve of an old long-sleeved shirt
- Wire
- Scissors
- String
- A small rock wrapped in cloth
- A needle and thread

Ask an adult for help.

1) Cut a sleeve off the shirt from the elbow.

2) Bend a piece of wire into a circle. It should be the same size as the bigger end of the sleeve.

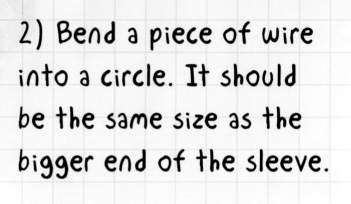

3) Put the wire inside the bigger end of the sleeve and sew it in.

4) Sew the rock in cloth to the sleeve, near the edge of the wire.

5) Tie one end of the string to the wire (opposite the rock) and the other to a branch. The windsock should hang freely.

The sleeve will point in the direction of the wind. Use a compass to find out what direction it is.

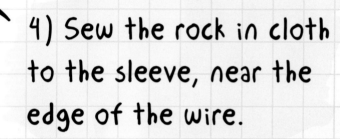

The Badge CEREMONY

Well done, you've made it to the end! We hope you enjoyed learning about weather – here's your badge to celebrate!

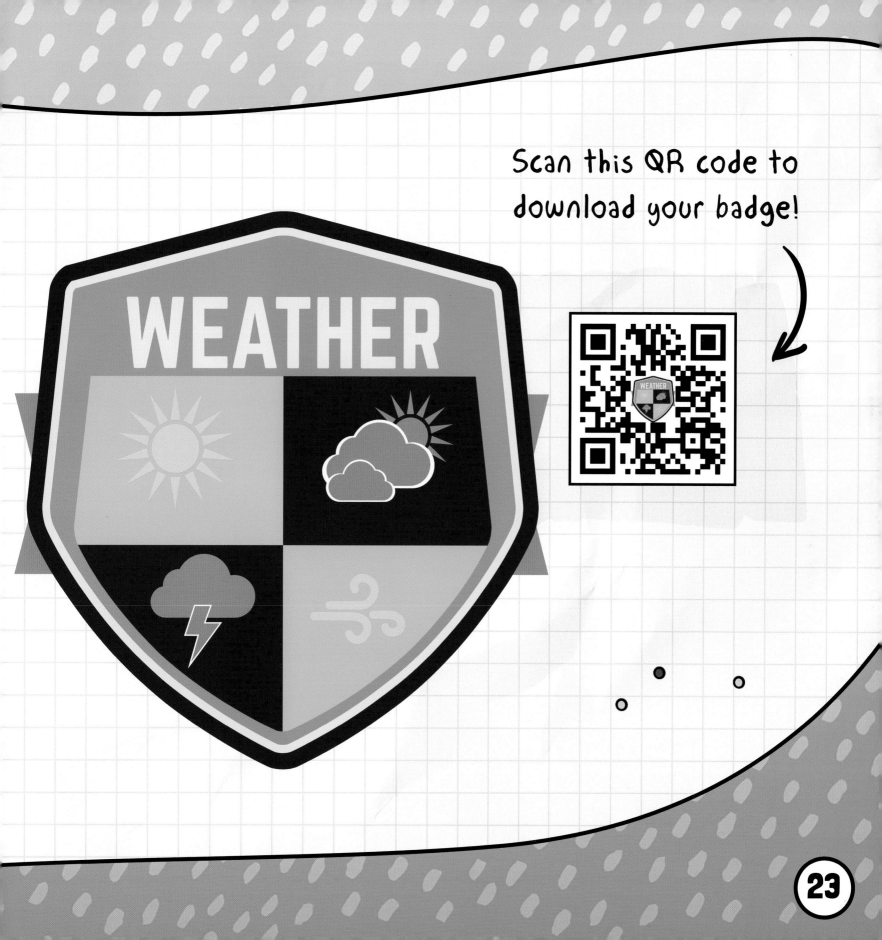

Scan this QR code to download your badge!

GLOSSARY

bloom	to produce flowers
experiments	tests done to explore and try new things
frozen	when a liquid has become a solid because of cold temperatures
habitats	the natural homes in which animals, plants and other living things live
hydrated	to have drunk enough water for the body to work
scale	a range of equally spaced values that are used for measuring something
static electricity	an electric charge that is typically produced by friction
tornadoes	storms with strong winds that swirl down from the clouds to the ground in a funnel shape
waterproof	does not let water through
weather forecast	a prediction of the weather that is likely to happen over a specific period of time in a certain place

INDEX